You Live

and

You Learn!

Written by Courtney Lande

A Special Selection of Poems

She's Written Over the Years

Throughout her Life

and

A Portrait of Her as a Person

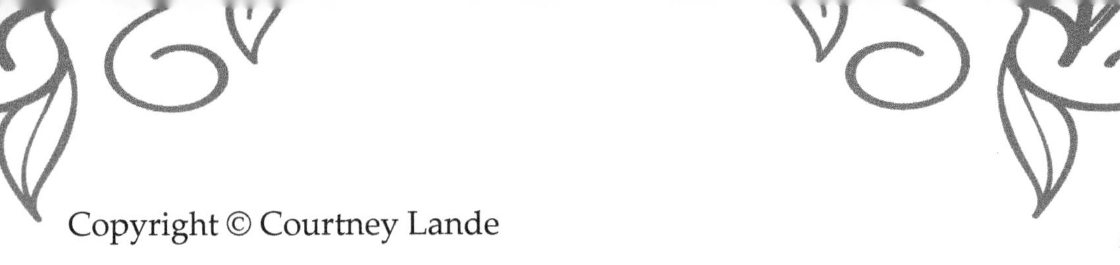

Table Of Contents

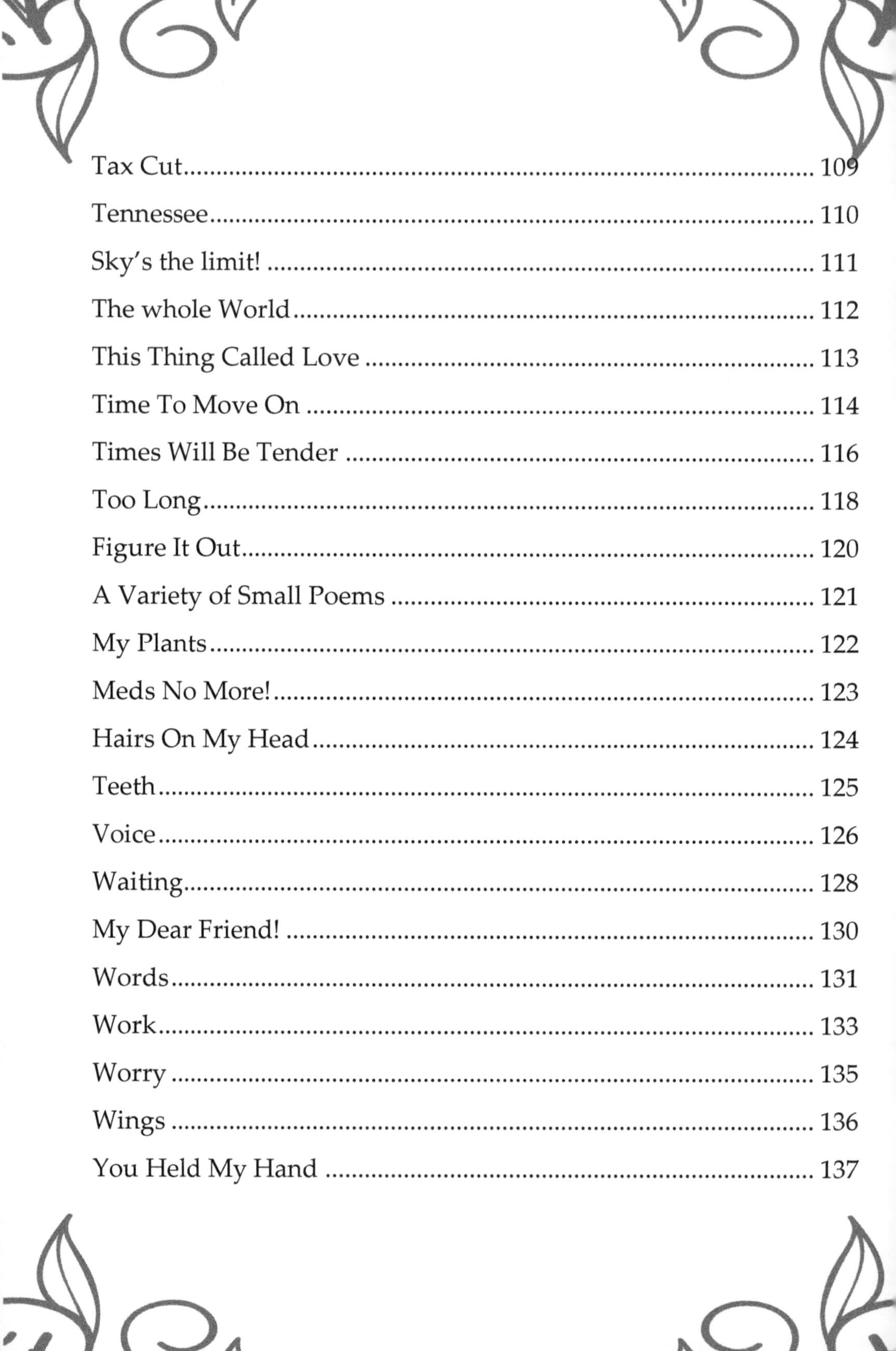

Jesus is Coming!

Jesus is coming

He's on His way

He's gonna be here any day!

They'll say it was aliens

That took us away

Deception runs wild

Leading people astray

Fearful sights—yes, you'll see

They will bring you to your knees.

When this takes place

In the coming days ahead

Remember all the words

In this book, I've said that.

Dedication

This book is dedicated to my precious Lord and Savior, Jesus Christ (Yeshua Hamashiach), who was sacrificed by the Romans on a cross and was tortured, ridiculed, and died. Three days later, He rose again. He sacrificed His life so we may have eternal life.

To the Holy Spirit, who is part of the Trinity that Jesus Christ (Yeshua Hamashiach) gave to me to dwell inside my body. My temple, which gives me the insight, direction, and help in every way.

To my angels, first my guardian angel, Michael, who watches closely as my husband and my two cats sleep. For their help in getting this book arranged and finished, I'm truly appreciative! Thank you, my special friends!

To my husband, Joe, and my two cats, Holly and Harley, who watched night after night while I arranged, typed, and finished this project. The support he gave and gives to this day—I couldn't ask for a better husband. Someone who loves me more than ever, and Jesus, too! The poems I've written—I have not experienced all of them, as I am an empath, extremely intuitive, and receive wisdom from above. I feel, observe, and study people. So, writing about life's experiences comes naturally for me, as I'm always trying to help people whether they ask for it or not. That has been my downfall.

Without all of you, especially Jesus (Yeshua), this book, and the others I've written and am publishing—I hope to publish until Jesus comes to rapture the believers, both Jew and Gentile alike. I'm going to occupy until He comes! Our Heavenly Father gets ALL the Glory, Honor, and Praise for everything.

1 Corinthians 10:31   Whether therefore you eat or you drink, or whatsoever ye do, do all to the glory of God.

Psalm 40:5 Many, O LORD my God, are thy wonderful works which thou hast done, and thy thoughts which are to us-ward: they cannot be reckoned up in order unto thee: if I would declare and speak of them, they are more than can be numbered.

Acting Like Fools

Loaded up my new car with several of my friends
We were driving to the party; it was around 10:00 p.m.
When we had arrived, music was playing oh so loud
People everywhere; it was a very large crowd.
Couldn't help but notice all the pills and booze you could find
People were shooting up; they were out of their minds.

Getting high and wasted, they all thought they were so cool
Deep inside, we knew better; they just acted like fools.
You don't need drugs and alcohol to fit in with the crowd
Stand up for yourself, make your own fun—do it, do it now.

The things that we saw going on, we all just couldn't believe
So, my friends and I decided it was best for us to leave.
The fun my friends and I all have is good, clean fun, I must say
Good music, food, games, and laughter—we wouldn't have it
any other way.
Going to a party at night or hanging out in the day
No need for drugs and alcohol for you to waste away.

Don't let anyone tell you that drinking and doing drugs is cool

Getting high and wasted, you only act like a fool.

There are so many ways to make your own fun

Go swim at the beach, play baseball, or run.

Join a football team, read a book that interests you

Find a new hobby, something you'd like to do…

Getting high and wasted and thinking you're so cool

What you're really doing is acting like a fool.

You don't need drugs and alcohol to fit in with the crowd

Stand up for yourself, make your "own fun," do it, and you'll
be proud!

Agree to Disagree

We must agree to disagree.

When differences come our way

No need to yell or even fight

It's the only way.

Yes, we can work this out

No need for harsh words

To scream and shout.

Let's agree to disagree

Communication is the key

Then we both will get along

Together, you and I.

Coming to conclusions

Always talk things through

Then we will figure out

On what we should do

Working out our differences
From time to time, it's true
You're still the one I wish to spend
My life with only you.

Angel

Divinely guiding me

Where should I go?

Showing me new things

Helping me to grow

My imperceptible friend

Only God sent

Giving me strength

That helps me to abide

Taught me about love

Stood by my side

Perceptions of new ways

A new way to see

You were always there for me

How lovely you are to me

Angel, Angel ever at my side

Watching over me

To you I confide

Angel, Angel, Thank you again
You are truly a Godsend

You watched and protected
Stood right by my side
Want to thank you again
How I thank you, my friend

To think I am never
Really alone in this world
You've been watching over me
Since I was a little girl

Blessed

My feet touch the ice-cold floor

Scurry down the hall, close the bathroom door

Brush my teeth, then take a shower

Fix my hair…

The train leaves in an hour

Still got time…

Pour my coffee

Turn on the news

Shaking off these winter blues

I smile anyway—yes, a brand-new day

"Thinking to myself," I say.

Have it better

Then most people do

Going to my job…

I enjoy it through and through

Yes, how grateful am I?

I ponder, I sit, and I sigh.

I am blessed; I am blessed
I am blessed, I know
A job, a family that loves me so
I've been blessed; I am blessed
I've been blessed, I know
I thank God above
Filling my life with much love....

My heart goes out to those in need
A job to put food on the table to feed
The less fortunate—a prayer
I say every day
To find a fulfilling job
One with excellent pay

Blind Date

I was lonely,

Then my friend had a plan

To set me up with someone

She thought I needed a man

She set me up with

Someone I didn't know

Thought I'd take a chance

And that I would go

A blind date,

Could this be

A blind date—is he right for me?

Could he be the one?

Looking through my closet

For something to wear

Can't find a thing,

Then there's my hair

What am I nervous for?

Is he short?
Is he tall?
I wonder what he's like
Could he be my type?
Oh, I don't know…
Does he drink or smoke?

I won't let my hopes get high
He might not be that special kind of guy
But I'll take a chance anyway; I'll go out and have some fun
Even if he makes me want to turn around and run.
Won't think about till death do us part
Although a good-night kiss could end up as a good start,
Stop and don't jump the gun, I remind myself and say
This is just a blind date anyway!

Blinds

I wonder what goes on

In his room at night

What he's doing now

If only I could peek through

His venation blinds

I only wonder how.

Sometimes I'll see

A crack of light

Shining oh so bright

Between 2 blinds it shines and shines

Only when it's late at night.

Peeping Tom, I'd say!

But look who's peeping too

Me, of course, I love to stare and watch

What can I do?

It can get very boring

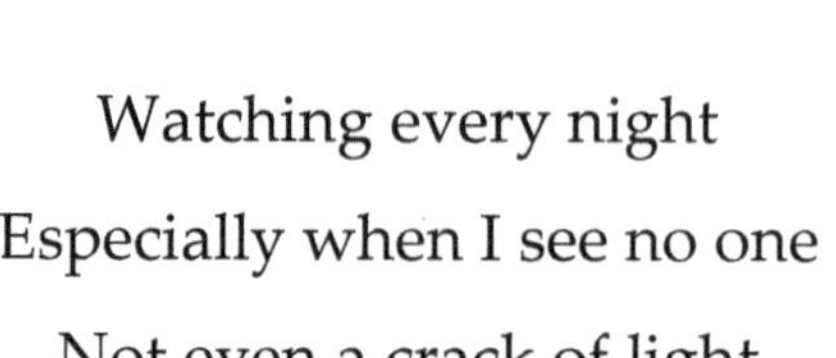

Watching every night
Especially when I see no one
Not even a crack of light

But oh, how I love to dream
About him, one day, being mine
As I peek again and again
I wish, time after time

Call You

We went our separate ways

I still think about the love we made

Don't know what went wrong.

The years have gone by

Still here, our favorite song

It's been way too long.

Way too long.

I want to call you

I want to call

Would you mind?

Would it be ok?

I want to call you

I want to call you today

Good times we shared

Laughed so hard we didn't care

I still love you

Yea, I still love you

Do you remember?

Places we have seen

It all seems like a dream

Seems like a dream

I'd like to try again

If it's not too late

Start anew

The love we once knew

I want to call you

I want to call you today.

Change Your Heart

We've been like sheep

Those have gone astray

We've turned on each other

In his own way

Don't need to speak

Words full of hate

Believe me when I say

It's not too late.

Change Your Heart

Change Your Heart

It's not too late to start

Why do you criticize?

Trying to hurt me deep inside

Whatever the reason

For targeting me

Because I am different

Don't like what you see

Words can hurt

And words can heal

Choose them wisely when you speak

Hate won't win—it's just a sin.

So, I may look different than you

It's my heart inside that counts; It's true

Dry

It used to be

A part of my life

No, not anymore

It just caused me strife

I saw what it was doing to me

It affected my friends

And my family

So, I closed that door.

Never to open again.

God gives me grace

He helps me along

If I'm feeling weak

He helps me stay strong

My goals are staying dry

I work at it each day

No, it isn't easy

That I will say

Straight as a pin

For all to see

It takes hard work

But I'm proud of myself.

Dry Spell

You don't get it; you don't fool me

You try to get into my good graces, I see

All too well I know the games that you play.

The words that you use

The words that you say.

Lovey-dovey words you use

Sometimes, only to confuse

Things will be different this time

That's all I hear you say

Trust me!

Another game you play

Intuition tells me to run while I can

As I think about it and wonder when?

You loved me once, then left me

Had realized what you missed

All the good lovin' that I gave you

My hugs and all the kisses

Now you wanna come back

Saying things are gonna change

When, in my heart of hearts, I know

You're really just the same.

Faraway Thoughts

The Day that I met you

My life really changed

Some things I've put behind me

Some things I've rearranged

I've put you in the center

And built my dreams around you

Yes, you mean so much to me

The special you I've found.

Before you came into my life

My skies were not as blue

Yet on the day you came along

The sun came shining through

Fish

Sometimes you feel

Down and out

Sometimes just want to

Scream and shout

We'll go ahead—just feel free

You could always talk to me

Confused, you may be

What to do next

Ignoring him might be

Might be best

If he continues to act

The way he does

Forget about him

My answer—because

You deserve to be treated

Like a Queen, can't you see

So, get out your rod

There are other fish in the sea

Forever Young

Life can be confusing

Not knowing what comes next

Being a teenager is hard yet fun

And that's what I like best.

Having friends over

Or going to a movie

Eating popcorn and candy

Boy, that sounds groovy!

Roller skating with your friends

Couples hand in hand

Dancing in the nightclub

Listening to the band.

Oh, us teenagers

Yes, do we have fun

We love to listen to music

And sing our favorite songs.

No, we never get tired

Having fun, the way we do

Older folks—they did it once

C'mon, how about you?

Forgive and Forget

Pain and anger

That you feel inside

Bottled-up emotions

You're trying to hide

Let it go

Just let it all go…

Forgive and Forget

Forgive and Forget

Forgive and Forget

All the sadness

You're still full of rage

I think it's time you

Turn the page.

Let it go

Just let it all go…

Forgive and forget

Forgive and forget
Forgive and forget

Reminding me of what they have done
It's not fair—you cry, you say they've won.
Forgive them, I know
Is what you should do
It's not for them. It's for you

Friend in You

She listens to drama

Madness in my life

The stories that I share

Pretends to reason with my doubts

The things I sometimes say

Shines the light so I can see

Misconceptions created

Acting foolishly

What would I do

If I didn't have the friend I have in you?

You mean the world to me

Can't imagine life

Without you around

The wonderful friend I found…. You

Friends

Someone to talk to

Any time of the day

Who you know will listen

To anything you say

They'll give you advice

They're there when you need them

More precious than a jewel or a gem

They're your friends.

Friends

Someone you can talk to

Friends

Who'll always be there for you

Through good times and bad

Happy or sad

Be thankful for the friends that you have

Some you grew up with

Others came along

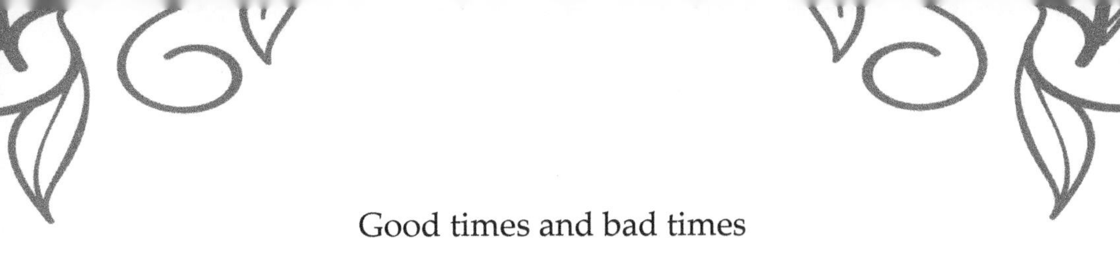

Good times and bad times

They love you right or wrong

Someone to go dancing with

Or to a football game

Life without one

Wouldn't be the same

Cherish all the memories

Of the Old Friends

You once knew

They hold a special place

Inside, inside their hearts too

Some you grew up with; others came along.

Gloves

All alone

I am standing in

The cold, dark night

Praying to God above

I don't get frostbite

Where are my gloves?

I left them at home

That's right

I was talking to you

On the telephone

Why did I forget them?

I knew I'd be out here

It's getting colder by the second…. Oh dear!

Last time when I forgot my gloves

I was out in a snowstorm

If I compared them to now

I'd say it was warm

Waiting out here is doing me no good

Think I'll go back home

Maybe read a good book

Handicap

Handicap, Shandicap

Who cares?

What really bothers me

The people who look and stare

They don't understand

They'll never see

This handicap doesn't prevent

Me from being me

Sometimes they'll whisper

All I could hear them say

Oh, that poor, poor dear.

Wish they'd just

Knock it off and leave me alone

I can manage pretty well on my own.

So, I took a few steps, and I fell

Look, I'm up again… told you I'm ok

Doin' better,

I think it's time you understood

No, this all wasn't planned

I can live with this, as others do

Can't you see?

I'm just like you

Head Over Heels

We've known each other 'bout a million years
We've come a long way through laughter and tears
Bet you didn't know, Bet you didn't know
The way I feel, the way I feel for you

Head over heels
Head over heels for you
I'm head over heels
In love with you
Don't know what to do?
Head over heels for you
Head over heels in love with you

Wanted to tell you, but I didn't know
I was too afraid of telling you so
Thought telling you would scare you away
I didn't know what I would say

I knew I'd fall in love with you

You captured my heart; you knew it, too

What was I to do but fall for you

I fell in love with you

Hold On

When it rains, it pours

Feels like another slammed door

It's like everything you touch

Seems to fall apart…

You feel like giving up

So, you pray for a change

Knowing deep inside

Things can't stay the same

Hold on, a door may have closed

Hold on… bet you didn't know

Keep your faith alive

Just give it a try

Better days, they lie ahead…

You wait and see.

Sitting at the bottom

You got to get up!

Can't see straight ahead

And your life becomes tough

Roll with the punches

That's all you can do

Pray for better days

You wouldn't feel so blue

Afraid, down, and out

Not sure of what to do.

Listen to your heart

Think things through

Our faith can be tested; yes, it's true

But better days lie ahead

Yes, I'm telling you it's true.

I Still Love You

Try to understand me

When I say that it's not you

I'm just a little down

And I feel a little blue

Please understand me

When I want to be alone

Maybe I need to think things through.

To shout or scream out loud

I, I, I, still love you

I, I, I, still love you

I'll get my head together

Feeling like myself

Ready again to face the world

You are standing by my side

Try to understand me

When I want to be alone

Maybe I need to think things through.

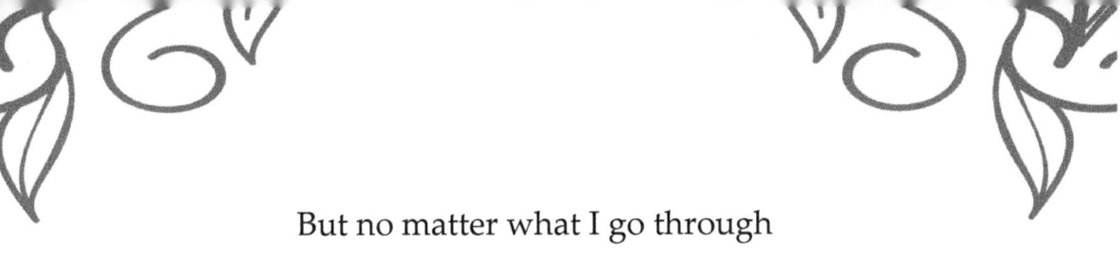

But no matter what I go through

I, I, I, still love you
I, I, I, still love you

I'd really like to share with you
Things that are on my mind
Right now I need a little space
Give me some room and time

When I get my head together
Feeling like myself
Ready again to face the world
You still are standing by my side

I'm the One

There's something you should know

I believe that we were meant to be

Maybe it's too soon for you to see

I've always prayed to God

I for you…and you for me

Take a chance

Take a chance on me

We were meant for each other

Can't cha see

Take a chance Take a chance … ON Me

Take a chance. Oh, Take that chance

Take a chance on me

Been too afraid to say anything…

Wondered what telling you would bring

I think it's time you should know

An intuition… I feel inside my heart

So strong that nothing would

Keep our love apart

I only hope and pray

God will show us the way

To explain the things to you, I'd like to say

If you'd only let me

Into your great big world

You'd see a woman

And not a girl

Jinx Josey

Jinx Josie, whom everyone calls

Whenever you're not looking

She stumbles, and she falls

What a klutz she is

Knocking everything down

There's a sign posted

Beware of Josey

Hanging downtown

I don't know what

gets into her

When she acts

the way she does

Sometimes I get this feeling

She wishes that she were

Not as clumsy as she is

And anyone can tell

But oops! There she goes again!

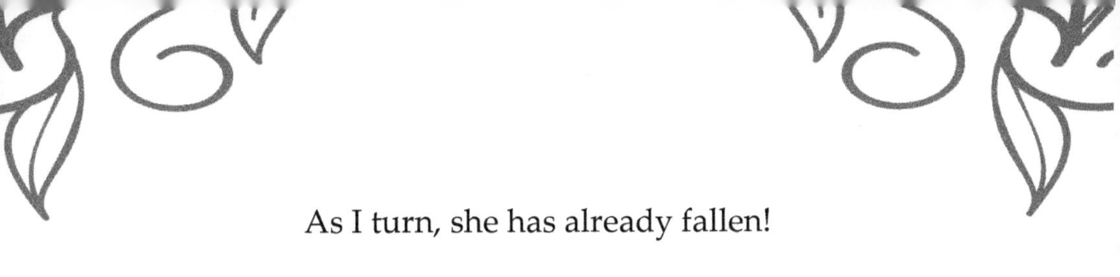

As I turn, she has already fallen!

Left, Right, Left

You got the right

The left

The right, left, right

And all they need

To do is talk, not fight…

Discuss the problems

Our Country has

Act like adults

Sit down and discuss

Our country's needs

Instead of Arguing

Who's right

Ohh, please!

This is a waste of time

It's not what we should do

We need to come together

Agree on a plan and see it through

Lessons

They taught me well

Taught me about life

Make something of yourself

Yes, they were right

Times can get tough

Money gets tight

Have faith in God

It's going to be alright

Lessons I've learned.

Like a Victim

The way it happened

No, it wasn't my fault

Yet you harbored anger

Like a victim of assault

No, it wasn't easy

Some days you would find,

Took care of me the best you could.

There were some difficult times.

Dealing with my struggles

Hoping you'd not see

Coming to accept what was handed down to me

Each day, I would grow

Though you took care of me, yes, I know.

Linda (who was Mom's coworker)

A toast of wine

Evening descends

An Exuberant smile she displays

Like rays emanating from the sun

Filling the room with warmth.

Cascades of laughter

Resonate through your soul

Inside your heart.

Her laughter rings through the hall

Down the stairs through open doors

Touching those that fall upon their ear.

Linda, so dear.

A gift with her, she brought

To freely give and share

Those truly loved by her

Graciously embraced

Times spent in her presence

Now cherished memories

Forever held in our hearts.

Lucky

Had too much to drink

Got behind the wheel of the car

Didn't occur to me to think

The mistake that I'd make is that I wouldn't go far

Driving 95 in a 55-mile-per-hour zone

Driving way too fast, I know; I'm just trying to get myself
home.

Couldn't see straight on the road ahead

It was getting late, and I should have been in bed

Not sure of the time; it all became a blur

I didn't see the sign; I didn't see the curve

Lucky how I made it, driving around the bend

Lucky how I made it, and my life didn't end

So foolish to take chances driving under the influence

While driving out of control, I had lost my senses

Should have known better than to get into the car

After downing too many, there's no way I'd go far

But all I could think was that I'd make it alright

Even after partying out all night

To take a chance and drive after all I had to drink

So wasted and confused, I didn't even think.

Thank God I've learned my lesson, a valuable one so true

Never again will I drink and drive, though it's something I
already knew

I thank God above for watching over me

When I was oh so careless and acted foolishly

I think I've learned my lesson not to EVER drink and drive

Could have hurt myself or someone badly. I'm so thankful I'm alive

Marriage Song

We thank you, Jesus.

Our Lord Above

For saving our marriage

Renewing our love

It was on the rocks

Many ups and downs

When we gave it to God

He turned it around

We knew we'd never

Leave the other behind

No matter what went wrong

Or what we might find

Our love is strong

Together we stand

We'll always forever

Hold hands.

Our vows were taken

Many years ago

A commitment we made

I'm so glad that we stayed… together

So glad that we're together.

Maybe

I never told you that I believe

You and I are meant to be

The intuition's strong, I feel

Resonates that this has to be real

Maybe it's too soon to see

I'm for you… and You for me.

I am too afraid to say anything

Wondering what telling you would bring

Maybe I'll let you know

I hope you stay and not go

C'mon, Take a chance on me

'Cause you're the one I wish to see

Hoping you will let me

Into your big world

And you'd see a woman

And not just a girl

Mismanaged Money

Mismanaged my money

Yes, it was true

I was way too careless

Wasn't sure just what to do

Bills piling high, had to pay

Where to find the money I need

Gotta get through this day.

So, I turn to God as I pray

Please help me through

This mess that I've made

There are people I need to pay

If you just help me

I'll do what you say

To manage my money

In a healthier way

Away with the card

And even the loans

I have it all to do to keep my happy home

Music and You

Thinkin' 'bout you all day long

Can't seem to get things done…

Ooooo, when we get together

We're gonna have such fun…

The times we spend together

I cherish all the ways

You try to make me happy

Each and every day

Good Music and you by my side

It makes me feel good inside

Puts me in the mood

Just thought I'd tell you, baby—Oooo

You call me on the telephone

To say I'm on your mind

That you want to see me

Do ya have any time?

That you're thinking about my kisses

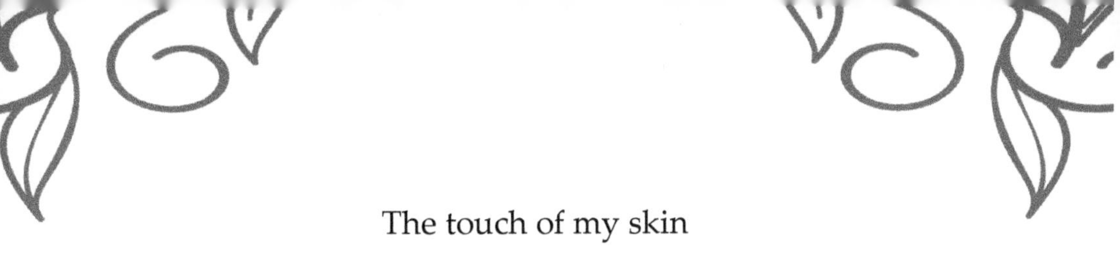

The touch of my skin
And you can't wait to hold me
While I let you in

When you whisper words of "I love you,"
Chills run down my spine
And your gentle kisses,
Sweet Caresses
Slowly, you take your time

So glad to be a woman
Feelin' like I do
Glad you're in my life,
'Cause I'm in love with you

My Husband

As I stand before you

And take my vow

Don't need to think twice

Or even wonder how

I would fulfill all my duties

As you take me for your wife

Where in this both together

Forever—that means for life.

Looking deep into your eyes

Such purity in your soul

You're the only one I wish

To spend my life growing old with.

I've prayed for you, my miracle

I've waited all my life

As I stand here before you

As you take me for your wife.

My Foot

I sit alone with my foot soaked in ice

Why didn't I

Say to myself or even think twice?

No… I had to do it

Go out dancing,

Spinning, turning, laughing, and prancing…

Sure, there's a price

You're gonna pay after falling

And landing on my foot

All I could hear was my mother saying…

Why couldn't you stay put?

Me… Naahh, I'm never in one place

Everyone I know

Can't keep up with my pace

Here, there, and everywhere

Everywhere I go

I get my kicks when I dance

Putting on a show

Yet as I sit here, foot frozen and all

I think about the next time

How careful I'll be

Not to fall

Oh, not to fall.

Pillow

My Pillow is all soaked

Losing sleep, the tears

Roll down my face.

Overwhelming grief

That's one more night

Feelings of despair fall

On this Heavy heart hurting

Yet I know

This too shall pass

I look to the skies

Is anybody out there?

Can't anybody hear?

Is anybody lonely like me?

Does anyone else fear?

Wish there was someone

To understand me, to hold me

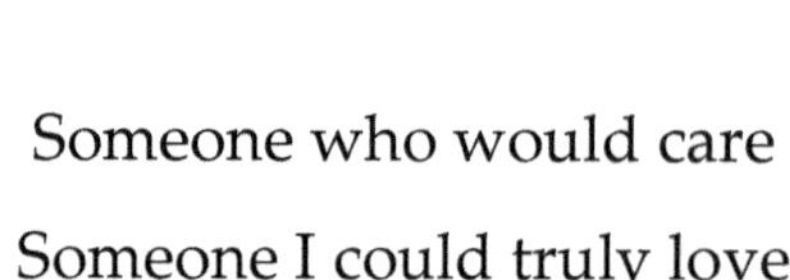

Someone who would care

Someone I could truly love

Nail on the Wall

Staring at the nail on the wall

Where the picture once hung

Before it came crashing down

Broken glass around me

I found someone

Who looks at me

The way I once looked at you.

A heart of gold he has

I knew He'd be

True, and best for me

Right from the start.

All you cared about

Was yourself

I knew in the end

We wouldn't make it.

Out with the old

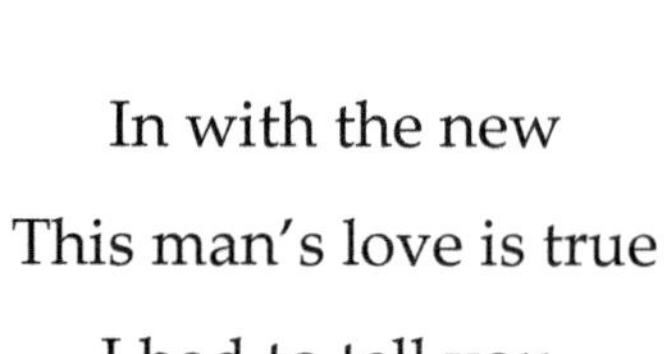

In with the new

This man's love is true

I had to tell you.

No more Tears

No more tears to run down my face

All because he said he needed space.

What a blessing! It was in disguise

I caught him in many lies

No more, no more tears will I cry

No more, no more will I wonder WHY.

No more, no more tears will I cry

Not me no more, Not I

Trust in each other; You're supposed to share

Come to find out, he never cared

Calling me his girl, I thought I was his world

I thought the only one—no, that wasn't so

Though I reminisce the days

They didn't last

Faded memories now

I leave in the past

Only Promised Today

They're gonna tell you it'll happen this way

Adrenaline, anxiety—oh, you *just* can't wait!

While waiting, you wonder, thinking it's all too late.

But how can it be when they told you your fate

Why seek to know what your future holds

You're only promised today

Why seek to know what your future holds

You're only promised today, promised today

You're only promised today

Nobody knows which way the wind will blow

Don't put your hopes in those who tell you so

Live your life only one day at a time

Don't seek out another to give you a sign

Set your mind free

From the weight of Anxiety

For nobody's future is secure

And that is for sure

Only God knows which way the wind blows

Open Your Heart

I cannot read your mind

When you don't share

How do you feel inside

You seem angry.

Is it something that I've said?

Are you saddened?

Do thoughts run quickly through your head?

Are you listening to me?

Baby, can't you see

C'mon, let's talk about it

Just you and me…

Open your heart

Let me inside

Open your heart

I won't run or hide

Open your heart, Open your heart, Open your heart to me

Open your heart, Baby, can't you see

Am I getting through

What's been bothering you?

It's been a while

Since I've seen your smile

Whatever it is you're going through

Just know I'm here

And we'll get through this…. Just you and me, baby—open
your heart to me

Anger and sadness are bottled up inside

Makes you wanna scream

Makes you wanna cry

I wish I could make all your problems disappear

Hold you in my arms and rid you of your fears

Period

Aches and pains

That's all I get

Moans and groans, I'm bound to fret

28 days and boom, it hits

Worst time of the month

Believe me, it's the pits

If an accident happens

And your pants are a mess

Could you imagine?

If you were wearing a dress!

Oh, how I wish I had started menopause

But the reason we have this

Is for a good cause

It's not good enough for me

When I'm in agony for four days

Every day

I wish we never had it

And it would just go away.

My Dad's Nickname Was Happy

I know for sure that

You watch over me

I can feel your wings so close

I cannot see you.

You let me know

It's of the utmost importance to

Learn and grow

In this big world

I'm still your precious girl

Remember… You tell me that

In person, you may not be

Open your heart and see

I'm still with you.

Haven't really gone far away

I'm so near

There's nothing for you to fear.

Everything reminds me of you

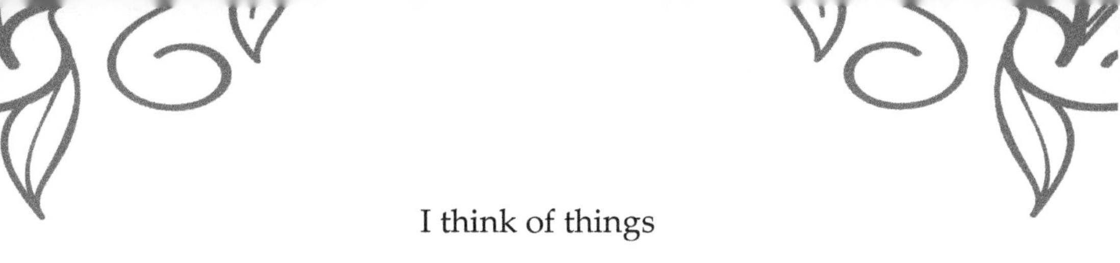

I think of things

You used to do

Sometimes it's too painful

Though I feel you watching over me.

It makes me happy.

You're really not that far

Just a twinkle like a star

Silly things you choose to do

Get my attention

Here's to you…

An object moved

Missing item found

Yes, you're still around.

Poetry, Skin, Holy Spirit Blessing on Me

God Bless my skin

That's oh so clear

And also wrinkle-free…

No acne scars, nor lines to see

I look just like a teen

That's what I'm told

Most every day

No argument from me!

They wonder, and they can't believe

They look at how this could be.

God bless my eyes

God bless my nose

My ears

My Gums

My teeth

God bless my spine.

My Blood, my bones

My head down to my feet

Holy Spirit

Please guide us

On what we're supposed to do

Holy Spirit, show us

For we put our trust in you

Holy Spirit, you are the only one

That makes our path so clear

We both truly adore you

And hope you'll always stay near. AMEN!!!!

Princess

Doesn't cook, doesn't sew

Ask her a question

It's probably no

Won't fold laundry

Or do the dishes

Gazes at stars

She makes her wishes

Driving her jeep

carries a cell phone

When you try to reach her

She's never home

Loves to go to parties

Dance the night away

Never runs out of things to say

Got brown eyes and brown hair

Ruby red lips, her skin so fair

Doesn't have a care in the world

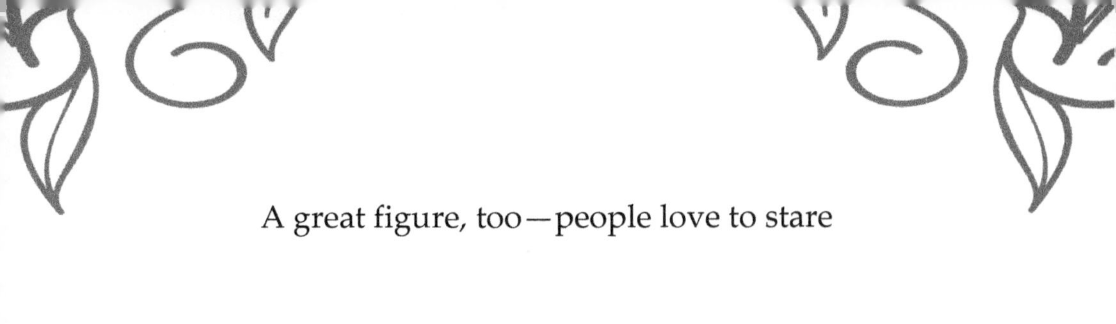

A great figure, too—people love to stare

Pump It

Aches and pains—that's what you'll get

Pump that iron, work up a sweat

Going to the gym almost every day

Since I got on the scale and saw what I weighed

I knew that I had to try to lose all this weight

So, I'd diet and exercise; it wasn't too late

Pump it, Pump it, Pump that iron

Working up a sweat

Just keep on trying really hard

You never will regret…

Work, work, work that body

It's never too late

Just exercise when you can

You will feel and look great

Running on the treadmill, leg lifts in the air

Had to burn those calories; I just didn't care

All that I desired was to look a certain way

Lose those extra pounds, so I'd work out every day

A couple of months later, after working out each day
I began to notice, and people began to say
A difference in the way I looked—they couldn't believe their
eyes
My abs became much flatter, and the flab came off my thighs
Gotta look good; want the others to see
Working out really hard, but I'm doing it for me

I want to feel good inside, instead of always trying to hide
Make better choices; eat healthy every day
Going to the gym, for me, is the only way

Relationships

Relationships that didn't last
They weren't worth my time
Then came you.
I've been hurt before
But I'm ready this time
To love again.

To bear my soul
All at once
You'd have nothing
To look forward to

If you'd just
Take your time
So early in the game!

Right and Left

You got the Right, the left

The Right, Left, Right

And all they need to do

It's talk, not fight!

Get in agreement

On what we should do

Get in agreement and see it through

Act like adults; sit yourselves down

Listen to our president.

Stop fooling around

Instead of Arguing Who's Right…

Don't listen to The Media

The ones that print Fake news…

Their purpose is to bring you down

You'll only sing the blues

This waste of time is not

Is not what we should do

We need to all come together

Agree on a plan…and see it through!

Rooftop

Before you came into my life

My skies were not as blue

On the day you came along

The sun came shining through

You were unexpected

Like a gift, for no reason at all

Like the changing of the seasons

Winter, spring, summer, and fall.

Happy days are here to stay

All because you came my way

When you smile and hold my hand

Lets me know you understand

You mean the world to me

Wanted you to know

I want to shout from the rooftop.

Tell you how I feel

Shout from the rooftop.

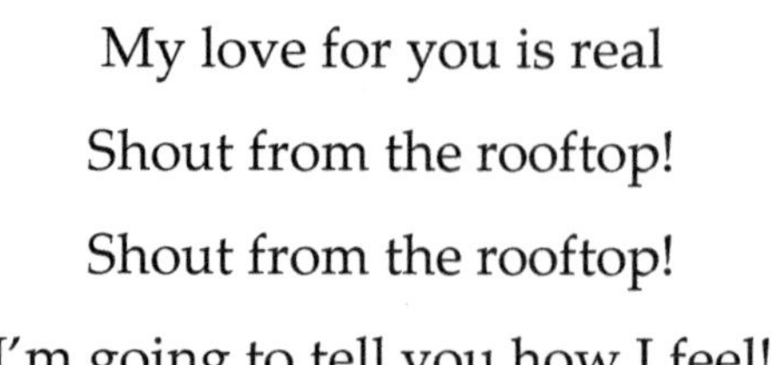

My love for you is real

Shout from the rooftop!

Shout from the rooftop!

I'm going to tell you how I feel!

Say No!

God will not call you

Into a battle you could lose

He'll give you his strength.

Intending all for you to use.

Helps you win the battle

Standing by, and with a grin

Watch, with FAITH, you come on top.

This battle you will win.

Setbacks

Setbacks

I will encounter

Along the way

It cannot be done

Is what most people say

Though setbacks

May depress me

And crush my spirit

I will refuse

To accept defeat

I will fight back

And not fear it.

Setbacks are temporary

I will get back on my feet

Walk with my head high in the air

Yes, God will give me strength

'Cause it is written… He cares

Pain such as this

It will pass the faith I will cling to

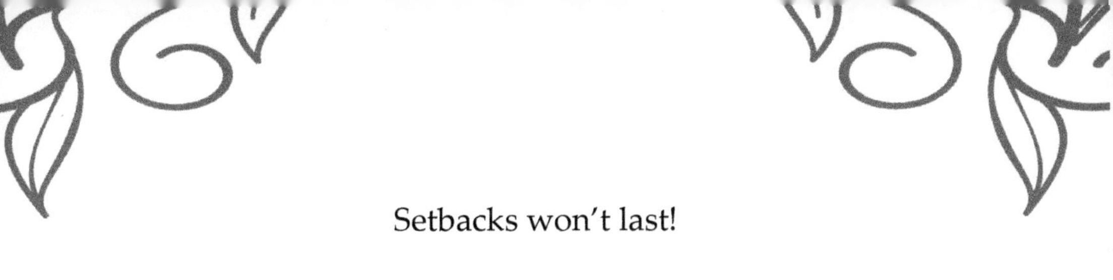

Setbacks won't last!

My friend, My Sister

She's more than just a friend to me

That much, I say, is true

If she wasn't in my life

I really wouldn't know what to do

We love and support each other

We think the same way

I trust her with my secrets

Safe and sound at bay

She's warm and very caring

Always ready to listen

There'd be something missing

So many things in common

Always there to lend an ear

Sometimes we sit in silence

Talk as long as time allowed

Yes,

Always there

This friendship is priceless

My sister, my friend.

Smiling

You got my attention

You caught my eye

I wasn't looking

When you came by…

Never expecting

You'd walk my way

So, I smiled back

Now what do you say?

You got me smiling.

Yea, I'm smiling.

From Ear to ear

Smiling, oh, smiling.

Wanna reach out and hold you near

Smiling, I'm smiling

As the day is long.

I hope this feeling lasts forever…

'Cause the feeling… is so strong.

You're a Blessing
You're a Blessing… in disguise
Came along…
In the nick of time…

The very thought of you
Brings a smile to my face
When you're near
My heart does race

Stars All Around

Stars all around

Hovering, I see

They manifest when you look at me!

Stars all around

Just want to break free

But at this moment

You've got a hold on me

Just the thought

Of our eyes meeting once again

I visualize, then pretend

I'm somewhere else… alone

Maybe walking on the beach

In this moment, your control

Your every reach

Stars all around

Hovering, I see

They manifest only when you look at me

Stars all around

Just want to break free

But at this moment

You've got a hold on me

Desire, I don't feel

My need is greater than the wanting

Feelings off is how I deal

You understand still; it doesn't change

Why am I here?

You only try to banish all

The fears I try to hide

Stranger

Don't listen

When someone tells you

I'll make you a star

Just come with me

Get into my car

They may promise you

The moon and the stars

Just turn a deaf ear

Don't get into their car.

Never get into a vehicle

With a stranger

Someone you don't know

Never get into a car

Don't trust it's OK to go

Don't go with a stranger

Someone you don't know

Even if they tell you

It's OK for you to go

Never go with Strangers

No matter what they promise you!

Strength

There were fists; He'd take a swing

Didn't care about you or anything

Called you names, put you down

While you would scream but not make a sound

Battered and bruised, you'd lie on the floor

Think to yourself, will there be any more?

Just wanted to curl up and die

All you could do is cry

You got the strength to get up and leave

You got the strength; you had to believe

You got the strength to walk out that door

You've got the strength; you walked out that door.

All the hurtful words that were said

Slaps in the face; you were hesitant

In leaving that place, leave it all behind.

Oh, a new life you'd seek and you'd find.

You got the strength; you walked out that door

If you had stayed, nothing would have changed

You'd get more of the same sadness and pain.

Strong

Dr. Jekyll, Mrs. Hyde

I used to feel deep inside

I'd go and laugh

Then hide and cry

Never understood

Or wondered why

Sometimes I once thought

of ending my time

It's not the answer, I know

We've got our share of problems

Young or old

Heard a voice just the other day

Took medication

Then it went away.

I've got to be strong

I've got to just hold on

Even if things are going wrong

There's always another day…

Yea, it will be alright
Going to win this battle
Every day that I go through life

I'll keep the faith and find my way
You may see me smiling
"Things are fine with me," I say
This I'm going to say!

Summer Days

The warmth of the sun

Permeates the air

Flowers they bloom

I see them everywhere

Oh, their fragrance

It tickles the top of my nose

As I breathe in their beauty

I'm filled head to toe

Children in the distance

They laugh on the playground

Others you see on the beach

Some swim in the sound.

Here we are together

It's the middle of June

Watching the birds fly

Calling one another

In their unique cry

Let's soak up the sun
This beautiful day
Making memories
To fall back on

Sunshine

You're always on my mind

I think it's time you knew

Words I long to speak to speak

'Bout how I feel I feel for you

Before I tell you how I feel

I have to I have to say

So glad you came walking by

Walking by my way

You're the Sunshine when my day is full of clouds

You're the sunshine; I'm tellin' ya, tellin' ya now

You're like sunshine—hmmm

You're like sunshine; you're like sunshine to me.

You brighten up my days.

So glad you came my way

My heart skips a beat inside

For you every day

I never thought you'd make me feel

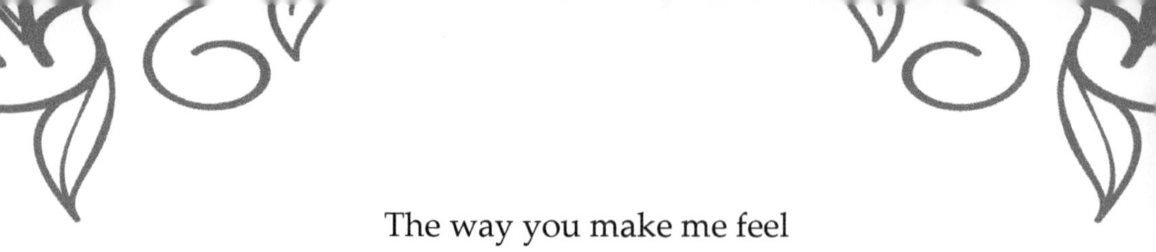

The way you make me feel

My heart skips a beat inside

Inside, it won't stay still

You're the Sunshine when my day is full of clouds

You're the sunshine, I'm tellin' ya, tellin' ya now

You're like sunshine—hmmm

You're like sunshine; you're like sunshine to me.

I knew there would come a day

When I would tell you anyway

It took me a while to say

You're like sunshine on a cloudy day

Sweet, Cute, and Kind

You're sweet, funny, cute, and kind

How I wonder

Would you mind?

If I told you I liked you

I'm glad we're good friends

Hope our friendship

Never ends.

Whenever you smile

You brighten my day.

So many things

I would love to say.

Yes, you already know how I feel.

Taken

I saw you try to catch my eye…

Don't want to lead you on

My heart belongs to another

I'm taken, Smitten

Another man, another lover

I'm Unavailable

Hope you understand

He's the only one for me

The only one

That won't ever change

So please let me be!

Take Time Out

No one ever listens

No one really cares

They never take notice

They're really unaware

I've been struggling with my talent

Looking for recognition

While they just tune me out

They don't even listen

Take time out to listen to me

Take some time out so you can see

Things I'm trying to do

You shut me out when I need you

Take time out to listen to me

Take some time out so you can see

Things I'm trying to do

Take time out to listen

A little praise now and then

Is all I ever wish for

Every time I practice

I am told to…shut…my…door…

With tears in my eyes, I begin to think of ways

To make them listen

I remind myself that they don't know.

They don't know what they're missing

Someday I'm gonna make it

I'm determined to never give up

You'll always see me trying

Competition—it could get rough

But God and I believe in me

I remind myself every day

Things'll only get better

No matter what they say

Talk

Don't close the door

Letting our love end

If we talk things over

I think it's time we

Let's work things out

We'll give it another try

I'd like to see you smile again

And I'd like not to cry

I don't want to close the door

Even though we've been through this before

We can't let our love end

It's time we talk again

I don't want to close the door

We can't let our love end

Let's talk things over

Let's talk things over

This can't wait another day

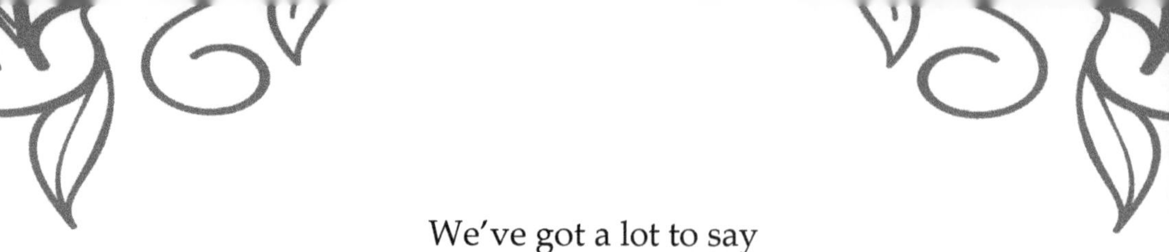

We've got a lot to say

I want to talk things over
I want to talk things over
How can I make you see…???
Pour your heart out … and talk to me.

Let's talk about it
What's on your mind?
I'd like to know
What you're feeling inside
I'll always love you
No matter what
Please don't run and hide
As I share my thoughts with you
To you I will confide.

Tax Cut

Oh Lord Jesus

Let this tax cut pass!

Please make this happen

Make this happen real fast!

You're the blessing we do need

The president, when he makes

In all that he does

Whatever it takes

8 years—there were promises

Promises never kept

Oh, those Democrats!

What a what a mess!

Jesus, can you come

Quickly, I might add

All of the believers in you

Boy, would they be glad!

Tennessee

We ask you, God

To sell our house

And move to Tennessee

Not to have a Mortgage

We both can live debt-free

We thank you, God

This is your will

To you we'll always pray.

At the right time

In the right way

Please guide us each and every day.

Sky's the limit!

The Sky's the limit

Make your dreams come true

There's nothing in this world

That I'd rather do

Then study my craft

Learn it inside out

Then share it with the world

That's what it's all about

The whole World

The whole world will tell you

What they think you should do.

Listen to me, they say

Believe me, it's true.

Why do you judge?

What's right for me

Why do you try

To make me see your way.

Thoughts now rearranged

Old patterns have now changed

New memories I now own

Wiser, I have grown

This Thing Called Love

I saw you there

One wonderful day

You took my heart

Then threw it away

That's why I ask the Lord

In heaven above

What is this thing called love?

Time To Move On

I'm looking forward, not behind, refusing to waste any time

On thinking about things of the past, things in life that did not last

Like you and me together so long, wondering now whatever went wrong?

Doesn't really matter; we ended it just the same

Too much drama, too many games

Can't look back on things that went wrong

It's time to move on, time to be strong

Letting go of the past, I will just start anew

Find a new love is just what I'll do

As I clear my head and rid my thoughts of you

Knowing in my heart the things I must do

Put away all the memories and make room for a new start

A new someone to come along, someone with a big heart

When the time is right, a new love I'll find

Someone who'll be there for me, a gentleman who's kind

Someone who would compromise, not give lip service, or tell
me lies

A man who's true in every way respects me each and every day

I'll never give up hope that my dreams will all come true

To find that special someone, a man who loves me too.

Times Will Be Tender

When faced with problems, yes, there'll be some

That doesn't mean you pick up and run

Complacent or tired, might even complain

The feelings you had might not feel the same

Times are gonna be tender; times gonna be tough,

There's gonna be times you want to give up

Times gonna be, Times gonna be Times when you just had
enough

We can't give, we can't give, we can't give up

Sit down and talk, 'bout what's on your mind

Rekindle your love, you will find

What brought you together? Dig deep in your heart

Remember the good days; it's a fine place to start.

Times gonna be tender Times gonna be tough

There's gonna be times you want to give up

Times gonna be, Times gonna be, Times when you just had
enough

We can't give, we can't give, we can't give up

117

Well, don't give up no matter what
Never give up, never give up

Too Long

We've been together forever, it seems

Then went our separate ways

Still reminisce about the times we shared

And all the love we made

Wishing you were here, still standing by my side

Can't shake the old feelings, the ones I try to hide…

It's been way too long

Heaven knows what went wrong

I just can't let the thought of you go

I still need you in my life; I just want you to know

If there's anything I could do to make you come back and stay

Just say the word while I sit here and wait

Why we're not together really puzzles me, as I sit and wonder
why—how can this be?

We're living two lives apart, alone, no longer a couple, separate
on our own

Another chance for us to make things work; I'll give anything to
try again

We used to be so good together, my lover as well as my friend

Remember all the good times that we both shared?
The fun and the laughter—we made a great pair
Would it be too much to ask to give our love another try?
I can't sit around and wonder why we're not together… Please,
let's start over

Think about the love we once knew; it felt so right and felt so true
If we only believe in taking the chance, we could both find true
romance
Second time around, we'll cherish each day
Express our love to one another in every single way

Figure It Out

Trying to figure out what to do
Still head over heels in love with you.

You treated me like a lady
Your gentle touch drove me so crazy
Now you're gone, moved away
Left me behind

Wanted to tell you
Miss the way you'd kiss me
Softly on my lips
The way you held me
Arms around my hips

A Variety of Small Poems

Jesus, please forgive me

For not listening to you

Instead, I chose to do the things

The things I wanted to

Oh Lord Jesus,

Oh, what a day

How we both thank you in EVERY SINGLE WAY

You saved our lives

Holy Spirit, Please

Keep our Government Open

And influence both sides…

Making them agree

As you open their eyes to see.

For it is Thy will to be done.

My Plants

Lord, watch over my plants

Keeping them all alive

They are so full of life

When you look at them, they thrive!

Meds No More!

No more Meds

I'll never, ever need

God Had Healed Me!

And that's what I believe!

Hairs On My Head

Grow the hairs upon my head

Where they should all be

Fill in all the parts

That may be sparse

For all to see!

Teeth

Keep my teeth strong

Keep them in my mouth

Where they all belong!

Voice

A voice I once had

Yearned again, I would speak

A doctor told me

A vocal cord was weak

Praying to God

Please give me the strength

To learn proper speech

And sing at great length

Exercising my cords.

Every single day

I had yearned to sing correctly

Many things I wanted to say

Before I knew it

My miracle had come through

I can speak and sing correctly

That's all I wanted to do

Our Heavenly Father

Is such a Great God

So full of wonder to me

How Grateful I am to him

For Eternity. Amen.

I'm so imperfect

But that's okay

'Cause I know you love me

Anyway

Waiting

I'm waiting and waiting

Your time is running out

No, I won't yell

I won't even shout

Get your act together

Do it very fast

All this contemplating

Will not last.

Is there another

Standing in Between?

You've got to choose between us

Gotta do it—and I mean fast.

We're both still in love

Things feel right

It's been so long

Haven't had a fight

Never doubt we'll make it

Through the good times and the bad

With Jesus, we will make it

With Him, so let's be glad!

My Dear Friend!

When we get together

All we do is laugh throughout the day

We never run out of things to say

She's the only one who keeps my every secret

Unique in her way

Very special to me

I can trust her and

Never have to worry.

Pretty eyes that dance

A smile that warms your heart

I could go on and on

Many places I could start

About my dearest friend

She's one of a kind, for sure

Whenever she's around

She'll leave you wanting more!

Words

Whatever the reason

For targeting me

Because I am different

Don't like what you see

Think I don't belong

Or even fit in

What is your problem?

You seem to embrace?

Like a thorn in my side

Invading my space

Look in the mirror

Do you love what you see?

Instead, you feel inferior

Always picking on me.

You make me your problem

Have to be in control

As you take your cheap shots

Yes, this too gets old.

No need to speak

Words of hate

Think before you criticize

Your aim is to hurt me deep inside

Words can hurt

And words can heal

Choose them wisely when you speak

I may look different than you

It's the heart inside that counts—that's true

Work

8 AM, sitting at my desk

No time for me to clean up the mess

I left back at home; got to answer this telephone

Bring the boss his coffee, then type a letter

God only knows when it will get better.

Working, working

Seems that's all I ever do

Working, working,

I'm thankful this is true.

Working, working,

Gotta be a better way

Turn my biggest passion into a job with better pay.

Bones are tired, I'm feeling weak

Sometimes I work 60 hours a week

I say to myself from time to time

I'm underpaid and half-alive

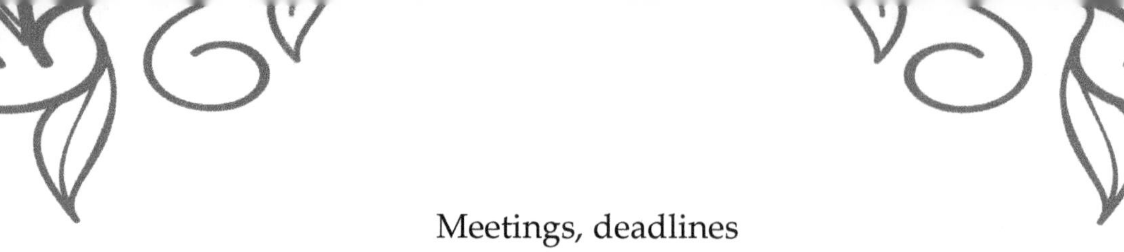

Meetings, deadlines
Can really wear you down
But you show up for work
Smiling, dare you frown?

When was your last raise?
Too many years, too long
But you stay… 'cause it's safe
And that's all you really know
You're afraid to make a change
That would force you to grow
So, a dead-end job—you stay
Till another comes along.

Worry

Paralyzed

Made-up fears

They may have haunted me

Afraid to look inside

What I might find

What would I see?

How foolish I've been

Created my own kind of sin

To worry.

Wings

You gave me wings

Taught me to fly

Waiting patiently

You stood by my side

Gave me strength

I never thought I'd see

You showed me

You do something to me!

You Held My Hand

Jesus, you held my hand

I was feeling down

Slowly, you turned

My world around

Telling me everything's

Going to be alright

To be happy again

Dance in the sun

Living, Laughing

Just having fun

When you took my hand

Things became clear.

You held me so tight

Drawing me so nearby.

With all you've done

All I could say

I thank God for you

Going out of your way

Eyes on Jesus!

All eyes on Jesus!

This is what I say

I keep preaching

I do it every day

Hope to fly

That's all I know

Time will tell

If I'm to go

Let's all repent!

Jesus is gonna come!

Sooner or later

For Thy will be done!

The Wedding Prayer

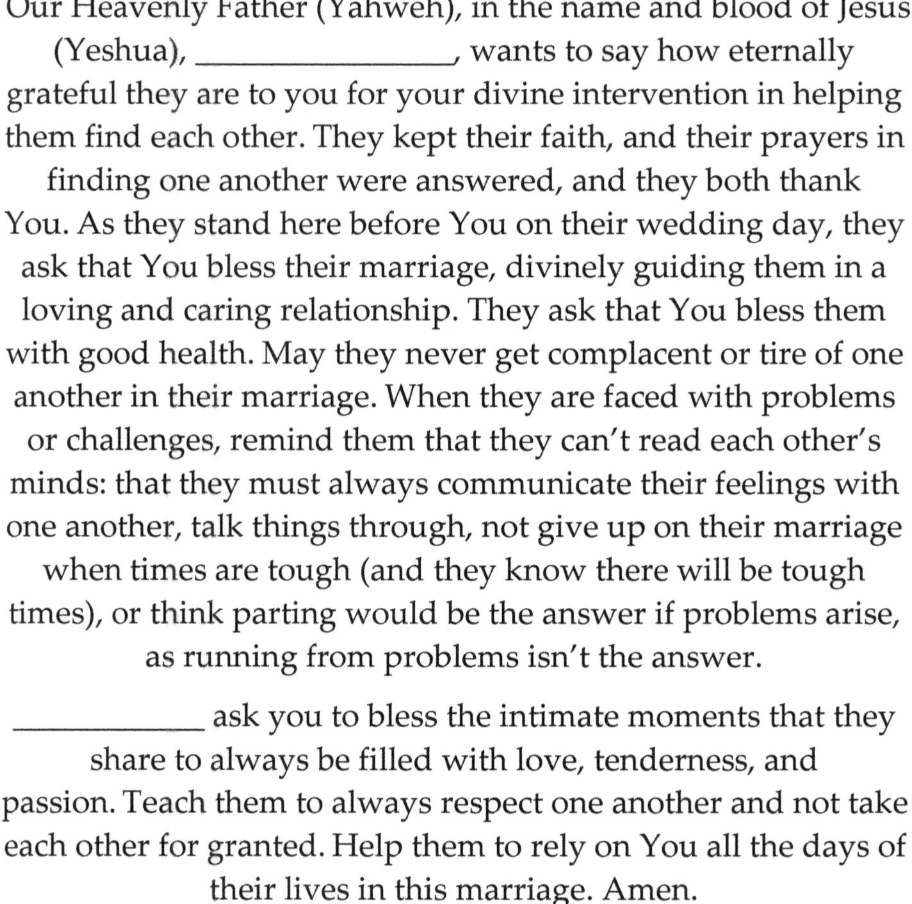

Our Heavenly Father (Yahweh), in the name and blood of Jesus (Yeshua), __________________, wants to say how eternally grateful they are to you for your divine intervention in helping them find each other. They kept their faith, and their prayers in finding one another were answered, and they both thank You. As they stand here before You on their wedding day, they ask that You bless their marriage, divinely guiding them in a loving and caring relationship. They ask that You bless them with good health. May they never get complacent or tire of one another in their marriage. When they are faced with problems or challenges, remind them that they can't read each other's minds: that they must always communicate their feelings with one another, talk things through, not give up on their marriage when times are tough (and they know there will be tough times), or think parting would be the answer if problems arise, as running from problems isn't the answer.

__________________ ask you to bless the intimate moments that they share to always be filled with love, tenderness, and passion. Teach them to always respect one another and not take each other for granted. Help them to rely on You all the days of their lives in this marriage. Amen.

GOD SAID:

Matthew 19:6   ⁶Wherefore they are no more twain, but one flesh. What therefore God hath joined together, let not man put asunder.

What God has joined together, let no man separate. So they are no longer two but one flesh. Therefore, what God has joined together, let not man separate.

About the Author:

Courtney Lande

Courtney Lande's life would not exist, nor would it be anything, if it weren't for Jesus Christ (Yeshua Hamashiach), as He is her rock and shelter in the storms of life. She owes everything she is and has to Him, her best friend and the love of her life, who means the world to her, as Jesus (Yeshua) gets all glory, honor, and praise for everything in it.

When she's not sharing the Gospel (good news) and love of Jesus Christ (Yeshua Hamashiach) and the Kingdom of God (Yahushua), she can be found going to thrift stores with her husband and afterward stopping for coffee or chai on the way home, a favorite she loves to do every now and then. Writing poetry and songs and dancing is her first love. She likes a clean, organized home, where she will cook and make up recipes as she goes. She loves to can, be it meat, veggies, or garden; loves music; and loves to sing. Researching the hidden things of this world is of interest, as is listening to various podcasts, whether from YouTube or the radio.

Courtney Lande shares her poetry and thoughts with the world in hopes for the next one to truly be a great change, with a great difference, that only our Lord and Savior Jesus Christ, true name (Yeshua Hamashiach), will do when he rules as King of Kings. Our current world is a hot mess, ruled by Satan, the "God of this world." He blinds the eyes of the unbeliever, and right now, we are nearing the end, as it seems. Biblical prophecy is happening faster than one can say "boo!"

I thought I'd compile all the poems I've written over the years in hopes of spreading a little joy and a little love to my fellow brothers, sisters, Earth Angels, Heavenly Angels, and what the heck:

While I'm at it:

THE SHAPESHIFTERS, and Aliens, the Fallen Angels—the ones who mated with the daughters of the sons of men, creating hybrids and giants that walked and still do on this current earth.

David Icke is a great author who writes about them EXTENSIVELY. Go check out his books!

Genesis 6: 4 There were giants in the earth in those days: and also, after that, when the sons of God came in unto the daughters of men, and they bare children to them, the same became mighty men which were of old, men of renown.

Jude: 1: 11 Woe unto them! For they have gone in the way of Cain, and ran greedily after the error of Balaam for reward, and perished in the gainsaying of Core.

Jude 1:14 And Enoch also, the seventh from Adam, prophesied of these saying Behold, the Lord cometh with ten thousand of his saints. [15] To execute judgement upon all, and to convince all that are ungodly among them of all their ungodly deeds which they have ungodly committed, and of all their hard speeches which ungodly sinners have spoken against him.

Where this gets interesting—and you never hear about this in most churches—I used to visualize myself holding Jesus' hand while going into hell and doing just this while driving to and from work for the last 13 years when I was employed, living on Long Island in New York. And lo and behold, I came to find out this was already written in the good book, and you never hear about this in most churches. Holy Smokes!

Jude 1: 21 Keep yourselves in the love of God, looking for the mercy of our Lord Jesus Christ unto eternal life. 22 And of some have compassion making a difference: 23 And others save with fear, pulling them out of the fire: hating even the garment spotted by the flesh.

Johah 1-10 And God saw their works that they turned from there evil way and God repented of the evil that he had said that he would do and told them: and he did it not.

1 Thessalonians 1:10 And to wait for his son from heaven, whom he raised from the dead even Jesus, which delivered us from the wrath to come! And He's coming soon! So, prepare yourselves, look for his coming as he says throughout scripture to Watch for him.

If the timing is off, and this isn't the end. I hope to write more!

The Bible says to occupy until Jesus (Yeshua) comes, so that is what I'm doing!

Thank you to all who purchased this book!

And my others so far:

"Normal"

isn't coming back

But Jesus is!

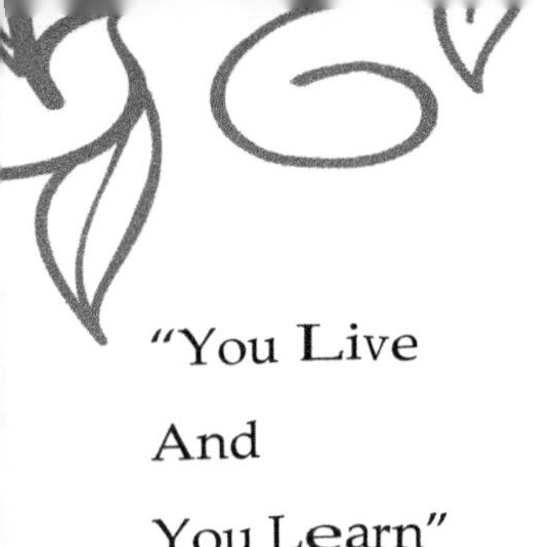

"You Live
And
You Learn"

www.ingramcontent.com/pod-product-compliance
Lightning Source LLC
Chambersburg PA
CBHW050029040726
47599CB00015B/1600